TOTALLY WEIRD
Rainforests

Contents

Tricky words are explained on page 32.

Journey into the Jungle

Are you ready to join an expedition into the amazing world of the steaming-hot rainforest, where it rains nearly every day? Trees tower high in the sky and amazing animals live everywhere — from the tops of the trees to their tangled roots.

That's weird

There are so many different kinds of rainforest animals that scientists haven't given them all names yet.

What's your name?

Where in the world?

Rainforests don't grow just anywhere. They are found in the hottest places in the world. These hot spots all lie near the equator, which is an imaginary line that goes round the middle of the Earth.

Leafy layers

A rainforest is divided into three layers. The leafy layer at the top of the trees is called the canopy. Below the canopy, smaller plants grow in the understorey. The forest floor is damp, dark and a bit spooky!

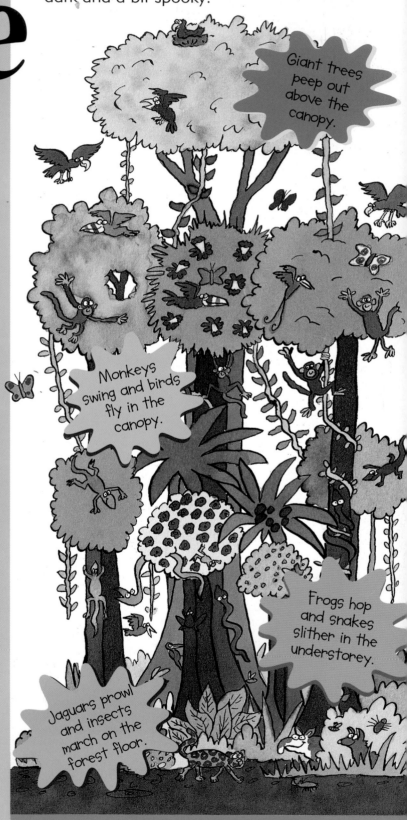

Giant trees peep out above the canopy.

Monkeys swing and birds fly in the canopy.

Frogs hop and snakes slither in the understorey.

Jaguars prowl and insects march on the forest floor.

▲ Each kind of animal has its own favourite spot in a particular layer of the rainforest.

▲ The Amazon river snakes its way through the huge Amazon rainforest, which is almost as big as Australia.

Life at the top

Birds that live in the canopy spend their time flying and squawking among the branches, stocking up on ripe fruit and nuts. Their feet never need to touch the ground.

Beak cool!

The toucan's enormous beak, or bill, has many uses. It's great for reaching those hard-to-get berries, slicing through chunks of fresh fruit and even for playing games of catch with other toucans. Its wonderful bright colour helps the toucan to attract a mate but it also warns other birds not to steal its eggs.

▲ A toucan's beak isn't as heavy as it looks. It's mainly a hollow shell.

Flower power!

From a lily big enough for a family picnic to a towering orchid — rainforest plants are extraordinary. Insects are attracted to plants by their colour and their scent, which can be sweet or sour.

High flyer

Rainforest orchids have inside-out roots. Unlike most roots which grow underground, this orchid's roots trail in the air and soak up moisture. The plant grows high up on the tallest trees. Its flowers are a hit with animals, especially insects, who drink its sweet nectar.

▲ This tree frog has found its own orchid swimming pool.

GREEN & GORGEOUS

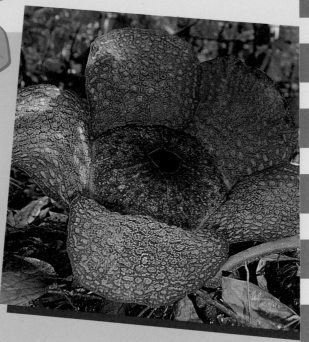

Record breaker

The prize for the biggest flower goes to the giant rafflesia that grows on the forest floor in parts of Asia. It can be as wide as you are tall, but it's no beauty. It has thick warty petals and a spiky centre that stinks of rotting meat. The horrible whiff attracts swarms of flies.

That's weird

Male bees flock to the bucket orchid to gather a gooey mess that will impress female bees. The male rubs it on his legs, then flies off in search of a hot date!

Yumm!

Feeling fruity

The durian is the smelliest fruit in the rainforest. Its stench of rotten fish drifts up to nearly one kilometre away. When the durian is ripe, animals sniff it out then feast on the stinky fruit. Many people think that the durian tastes delicious, too.

The bubble gum you blow into bubbles is made from chicle, which comes from sapodilla trees in the Amazon rainforest.

Rubber starts off as a milky juice which flows from a rubber tree. But it ends up as bouncy, stretchy material, perfect for making all kinds of things, from footballs and bicycle tyres to wet suits.

7

Animal chatters

Rainforest animals have plenty to talk about. Frogs croak, monkeys whoop and birds screech, which is their way of saying 'Hi!' to friends and 'Get lost' to enemies.

Strange but true

The tiny poison dart frog is just over one centimetre long. That's the size of a small grape.

Frog chorus

All kinds of male frogs serenade female frogs with deep throaty croaks. The male with the loudest booming croak wins the affection of the female. Frogs also croak to tell enemies to hop off!

Crrroak!

How much louder do I have to be?

▲ This frog can stretch the skin under its chin like a balloon to make a mega-loud croak!

A nose for noise

The male proboscis monkey has a long droopy growth for his nose, which he 'plays' loudly like a trumpet. He lets other monkeys in his group know that he's boss by warning them of danger and calling them together for meetings.

Tuneful gibbons

Gibbons are musical animals. When male and female gibbons mate, they stay friends forever and sing duets to one another. A family of gibbons also calls across the canopy to keep other families away from its patch.

Rainforest animals have some strange ideas about setting up a home and starting a family. Most leave their young to look after themselves, but a few take great care of their babies.

Forest families

BACHELOR BIRD HOUSE

The male bower bird makes a fancy house with matching flowers and feathers to attract a female bird.

> This spot is just perfect.

Then he adds a splash of colour with berry juice.

SQUASHED BERRIES

> I like this shade of blue.

When the house is ready, he waits inside for a female bower bird.

> Cool place to live!

> Well, hello!

Strange but true

Chimpanzees live in close-knit families. They groom each other's fur, hold hands and even kiss each other!

Gorilla picnic

Each morning, the father gorilla, called the silverback, wakes up the family to enjoy a meal of fruit, leaves and bark. After breakfast, the grown-ups snooze while the young play games. The young gorillas will stay with their parents until they are more than ten years old.

▼ A mother sloth hangs upside down from a tree by her toes. Her baby holds on tight.

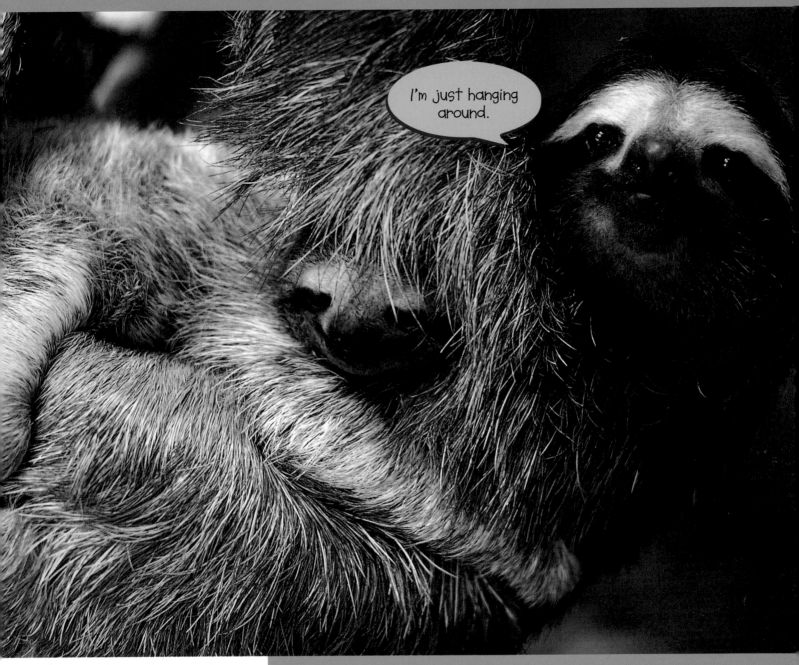

I'm just hanging around.

Lazy baby

There's no pressure on a baby sloth to leave home. Each long-haired sloth baby spends six to nine months hanging on to the fur on its mother's stomach. Then the lazy-bones moves off on its own, extremely slowly, to find its own tree, where it may live for years and years.

Hey, Dad just swallowed the kids!

Being a dad is a serious business for the male Darwin's frog. When the eggs hatch into tadpoles, he scoops them up and carries them around in a pouch in his mouth. After about three weeks, the proud dad spits out the little froglets, who can now hop around by themselves!

Fruits of the forest

What's on the menu in the rainforest? Many animals like to gobble up crunchy insects and other scrumptious creatures. But there are also plenty of vegetarians who munch only leaves, shoots, fruit and nuts.

Strange but true

A gorilla treats itself to breakfast in bed. It just lies back in its grass nest and picks fresh green leaves from nearby.

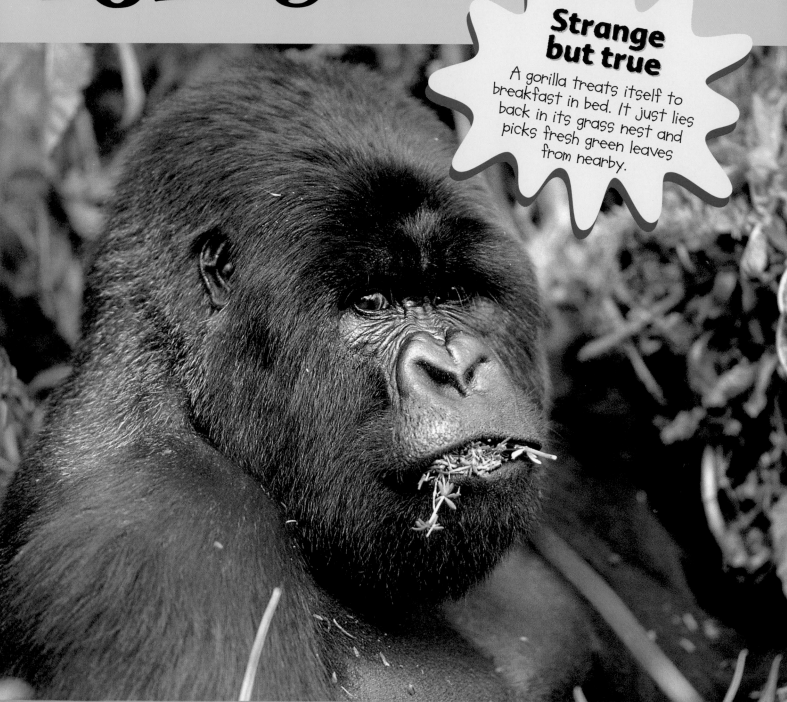

▲ A gorilla has a massive appetite. Every day, this vegetarian spends six hours eating.

If I don't find my food, I'm going to go nuts!

Jaw-some!

An agouti is a champion nut-cracker that has incredibly strong jaws. It is one of the few animals that can crack the tough Brazil nut. The agouti is similar to other rodents because it buries a hoard of nuts to save for later. But the forgetful creature can't always remember where it put them! The lost nuts often sprout up later and grow into trees.

HOME-GROWN LUNCH

Phew! I need a holiday!

Leaf-cutter ants work in teams to grow food. One team collects leaves.

Your turn now!

Another team chews the leaves until they turn into a sticky pulp.

Tasty fungus grows on the pulp. The ants all feast on the fungus.

Mmm, fungus. My favourite!

Cats go fishing

Jaguars are the only big cats that live in Central and South America. Unlike many cats, jaguars are happy in water and are strong swimmers. They enjoy eating fish and sometimes even catch crocodiles. They also eat smaller mammals. Jaguars are good climbers and often hide in leafy trees, waiting for their next meal to stroll by. Then they jump down and give their victim a nasty surprise.

That's weird

Most insects eat plants, but with the pitcher plant it's the other way round. An insect slides from the rim of the plant into a pool of liquid and drowns. Then the pitcher plant digests it.

13

Gotcha!

▲ A chameleon glues a victim to its long tongue with a sticky glob of spit! Yuck!

Crafty chameleon

SNACK ATTACK

In a fraction of a second, the quick-draw chameleon snaps up a tasty insect. The chameleon's tongue is as long as its body!

A chameleon's tongue ▶ can be this super-long!

0 cm 1 2 3 4 5 6 7
0 inches 1 2

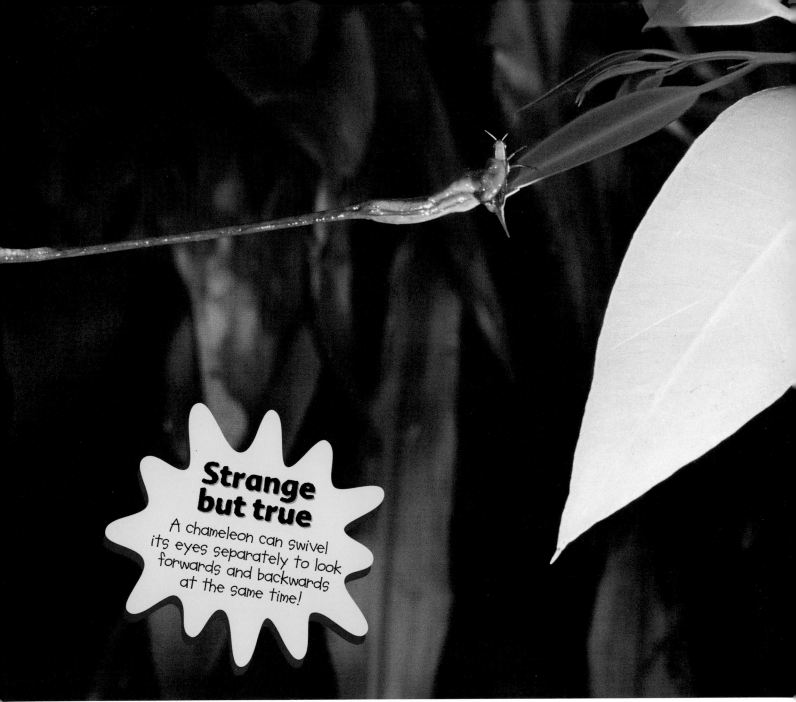

Rainbow reptile

Imagine being able to change colour! In minutes, a chameleon turns from one colour to another to blend in with its surroundings and to hide from enemies. It also changes colour with its mood. An angry chameleon comes out in orange patches to let other chameleons know that it's cross.

For my final trick!

When all else fails, the chameleon has one last trick to fool enemies. It plays dead. When face to face with danger, it flops to one side, with a limp body, drooping eyelids and stiff legs. As soon as its enemy turns its back, the chameleon makes a dash for it.

Did that twig just move? Did that leaf just fly away? Rainforest animals are masters of disguise. They have all kinds of tricks to help them catch dinner and to avoid being eaten themselves!

That's weird

An orchid mantis is patient and cunning. It looks just like an orchid gently swaying in the breeze. When an insect lands nearby, it pounces.

Bottoms up!

When this eyespot frog feels threatened, it shows its attacker an eyeful of the black circles on its bottom. The frightened attacker backs off because it thinks that the circles are the eyes of a much larger creature!

Vanishing act

The ornate orb-weaver spider flattens itself against the bark of a tree, stays absolutely still and – hey, presto – it seems to disappear. The spider's colouring exactly matches the mouldy, flaky and mottled colours of the bark.

camouflage

Tell me why

RAINFOREST ANIMALS ARE COPYCATS

The spiky thorn bug looks just like a genuine prickly plant thorn, so most enemies leave it alone.

Strange but true

A gecko can't blink so it uses its tongue to wash its eyes.

The walking-stick insect is an experienced actor. It blends in with its surroundings and, if necessary, won't move for up to six hours!

▲ Look closely. Can you make out the bulging eyes of the gecko lizard? Its patchy green and brown skin looks just like bark.

Danger!
Red alert

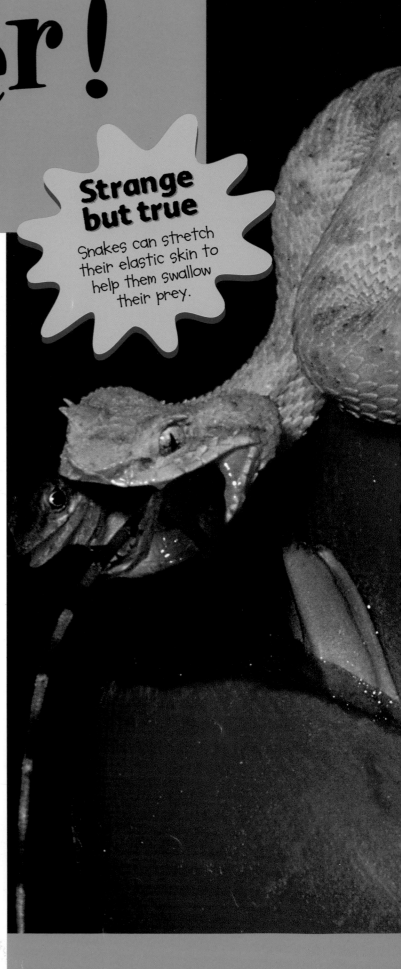

There are always watchful predators about, ready to fight to the death. Many have ingenious ways of catching their prey. They may trap, poison, bite or even strangle it. Or they may just swallow it up alive.

That's weird

An ogre-faced spider weaves a web about the size of a postage stamp and waits in ambush. When an insect zooms by, it covers it with the sticky net and delivers a lethal bite.

Viper swipe!

The eyelash viper fixes its eyes on its target, rotates its fangs at the front of its upper jaw into position, aims, then bites with deadly accuracy. It injects lethal poison straight through its fangs into the prey.

18

Flying killers

An eagle is the biggest and fastest flying killing machine in the rainforest. It can spy a monkey in the canopy from more than three kilometres above, swoop down at lightning speed and snatch it with its razor-sharp talons. Then it flies away to enjoy its meal in peace.

Dinner-time!

Stranglehold

The anaconda is a giant snake that can grow as long as six children lying end to end. It wraps its long body round and round its victim, then squeezes tight. The victim can't escape and soon chokes to death.

▲ In double-quick time, the tiny eyelash viper's head darts forwards to grab a passing lizard in its big mouth.

19

Lethal mini-beasts

Many of the deadliest killers in the forest are also the smallest. Insects and spiders are top-notch hunters that catch their prey in all kinds of disagreeable ways.

Strong stink!

The rove beetle has a smart but smelly disguise. It looks like a piece of dung! It hangs around real dung, where it gobbles up flies which are drawn to the honking stuff. And when there's no dung around, the beetle makes its own stink to lure flies to their doom.

Believe it or not

Some insects use chemical warfare by spraying enemies with blistering liquid.

Slurping spiders

A black widow spider is enemy number one to insects. Its venom can be 15 times more deadly than that of a rattlesnake. One small nip from a black widow's needle-sharp fangs and it's all over for an insect. Then the spider sucks out the insect's insides for a tasty treat.

WASP VERSUS TARANTULA

The female hawk wasp is a small but daring opponent of the tarantula spider. She dives in bravely.

I must avoid those fearsome fangs!

The wasp injects venom into the spider so that it cannot move, but is still alive. Then...

Ouch! You bully!

...she drags the spider to her nest and lays eggs on it. When the eggs hatch, the baby wasps eat the spider.

Phew! Winning is hard work!

The praying mantis claps together her two front legs to grip her unfortunate victim.

Munching mantis

The female praying mantis is a calm and calculating killer. She sits extremely still, holding up her front legs as if saying a prayer. But this devious insect is really waiting for a tasty morsel to fly by. The praying mantis is so greedy that she sometimes gobbles up her partner after mating!

What's in a name?

Battalions of army ants march like real soldiers in search of food. They are fierce hunters that capture and kill.

Batty bats
AT HOME

Bats are amazing. They are mammals, like you, but they can fly. When these acrobats of the air pause for rest, they nest together in big groups.

▲ During the day, tent bats snuggle up together, resting in preparation for night flights when they search for fruit and insects.

Tree-houses

Tent bats camp out in the understorey near fruit trees. The bats make cosy, hanging tents from large leaves. First the little nibblers bite small holes along either side of the leaf. This bends the leaf to make a roof shape. Then they hook their feet into the holes and hang, heads down, safe from the heat of the sun and out of the wet of the rain.

That's weird

Fruit bats have their own air-conditioning system. They fan themselves with their big, flappy wings!

This is cosy!

Life's a breeze...
swinging in the trees

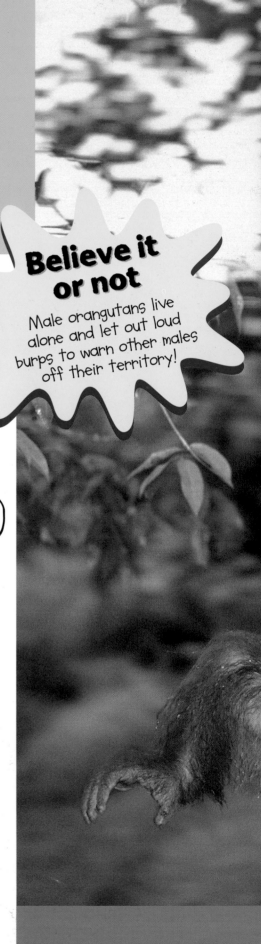

The canopy is full of animal acrobats and trapeze artists. Monkeys, frogs and snakes leap from tree to tree with incredible ease. They seem to fly through the air — bobbing and tumbling, but never losing their balance.

Believe it or not

Male orangutans live alone and let out loud burps to warn other males off their territory!

FLYING SSSSNAKES

Where's that frog going?

A slippery snake slithers and wriggles, then jumps after its prey.

It curves itself in an S-shape and soars through the air. The chase is on.

I'm behind you!

It lands safely on a branch. Gulp!

Branching out

Monkeys are graceful tree acrobats. They stretch and swing, gripping on to branches with their strong hands and feet. An orangutan can soar huge distances between one branch and the next. But a big, old male orangutan is too heavy to live in the trees, so he retires to the ground and moves on all fours.

Super glue

Tree frogs have real suction power. Their special fingers and toes stick to slippery tree trunks and branches. They are so sure-footed, they can hang upside-down from a branch without falling off.

Going up

Scientists who study animals in the rainforest need a head for heights. They use climbing ropes, walkways and even hot-air balloons to make sure they get a bird's-eye view of what's going on in the treetops.

Squawk!

▲ An orangutan has much longer arms than legs!

In the Swim

Huge rivers, such as the mighty Amazon, flow through every rainforest. If you take a peek below the surface of these murky waters, you'll see some creatures that are wonderfully weird!

It's shocking!

An electric eel's muscles work like batteries. They make electric signals, which help the eel to find its way around the muddy river and stun its prey. It can zap its victims with up to 650 volts – enough electric power to stun a horse!

I like my fish fried!

Believe it or not

A crocodile has a pair of see-through eyelids that protect its eyes while they are still open.

Open wide

A crocodile's huge jaws and sharp teeth would scare any dentist. This ferocious reptile lurks with only its eyes and nostrils above the water, waiting for a thirsty animal to come for a drink. SNAP! It opens its huge jaws and the unfortunate creature is dragged under the surface to a grisly death.

What's in a name?

The mudskipper jumps and skips along the muddy shores on strong pectoral fins. It's just as happy living underwater, too.

Gentle giant

What eats a vast amount of plants each day and looks like a swimming elephant? The manatee. It's the largest rainforest animal and scientists think that it really is a distant relative of the elephant. It swims slowly using its flippers and tears at plants with its long lip.

Under the microscope

The piranha fish has rows of needle-sharp teeth. It smells the blood of an injured animal, chases it, then rips it up!

▲ A manatee knocks sand off a plant with its amazingly long lip and then swallows it whole.

HA HA! How do electric eels get to school? They take a buzz. **HEE HEE!**

After dark

The rainforest is open 24 hours a day. When darkness falls, the night-shift takes over as wide-eyed animals wake up and come out to play!

Hey! It's rude to stare!

▲ A bushbaby's big eyes and excellent hearing help it to find insects and other food at night.

Gaping gecko

It's easy to lose your way in the dark. Many nocturnal animals, including geckos, have large eyes that let in lots of light. In the daytime, their eyes become narrow slits.

Success story

A firefly makes light work of finding a mate in the dark. It has a light in its tail that flashes on and off as a mating call!

The heat is on!

The pit viper cannot see well in the dark, but that's not a problem when it comes to finding prey. It has special organs in its head that sense the warmth of a living body. It just follows the heat to its next meal.

Bats work the night-shift looking for food. The blood-thirsty vampire bat bites birds and mammals with its two sharp front teeth. Then it laps up blood from the gaping wounds!

In the dark of night, the fishing bat spots a fish's fin sticking out of the water. It keeps tabs on it with a special tracking system. When the bat is close to the fish, it pounces on its fresh supper.

29

Prize day

It's prize day in the rainforest and you have a chance to meet even more amazing plants and animals. Some are huge and some are tiny, but every one's a winner!

Fearsome froggy

The prize for the scariest animal goes to the poison dart frog. It looks harmless, but this frog is one of the deadliest creatures around. Some have enough poison in their skin to kill 50 snakes.

What a mouthful

The goliath bird-eating tarantula beats all other spiders for size. Measuring as much as 28 centimetres from toe to toe, this hairy bird-eater fits nicely across a large dinner plate. Imagine finding this giant spider on the table instead of your lunch. Eek!

Beetle that

The gold medal for weightlifting goes to the rhinoceros beetle. This colossal creepy-crawly is so strong, it simply lifts up other insects that get in its way, using its pointed horns.

Wonder wings

You can hardly miss the Queen Alexandra's birdwing in a butterfly parade. The female's wings can measure an incredible 28 centimetres from tip to tip, making it the largest butterfly in the world.

actual size

Teeny weeny

Here's a bird that's a champion featherweight! The tiny bee hummingbird of Cuba weighs in at a record-breaking 1.4 grams, which is too light even to register on a kitchen scale. This tiny tweeter is also a star gymnast. It can fly backwards, sideways and upside down, or just hover on the spot.

Creepy climbers

Rattan plants from Southeast Asia are at the top of the class for climbing. They grow along the ground and crawl up tree trunks, stretching to a height of more than 152 metres. That's one and a half times taller than the Statue of Liberty!

Index

Author: Kate Graham
Consultant: Jonathan Elphick
Illustrations: Woody, Lorna Kent
Photographs: Cover: Images Colour Library; p3: Robert Harding Picture Library; p4/5: Robert Harding Picture Library; p6: Tony Stone Images; p7: Bruce Coleman Ltd; p8/9: Still Pictures; p9: FLPA; p11: Bruce Coleman Ltd; p12: Planet Earth Pictures; p14/15: Natural History Photographic Agency; p16: Premaphotos Wildlife; p17: Bruce Coleman Ltd; p18/19: Michael & Patricia Fogden; p21: Natural History Photographic Agency; p22/23: Bruce Coleman Ltd; p25: Tony Stone Images; p26: Natural History Photographic Agency; p27: Planet Earth Pictures; p28: Robert Harding Picture Library; p29: Premaphotos Wildlife; p30: Bruce Coleman Ltd; p31: The Natural History Museum, London.

Published by Two-Can Publishing, a division of Zenith Entertainment plc, 43-45 Dorset Street, London W1H 4AB

Created by Two-Can Design Ltd, 346 Old Street, London EC1V 9RB

ISBN: 1-85434-793-4
Dewey Decimal Classification 574.5
A catalogue record for this book is available from the British Library.

Paperback 10 9 8 7 6 5 4 3 2 1

Printed in Hong Kong by Wing King Tong